Did you know that the word tractor means, "to pull".

A tractor is a strong work vehicle used for farming.

Tractors can be used to pull implements or trailers and can carry and lift things too.

Every farmer needs a tractor on their farm.

Let's look at Tractors

Tractor

A tractor is made up of different parts. The most important part of the tractor is the powerful engine underneath the bonnet.

Let's look at some other parts...

Exhaust
The exhaust carries gas out from the engine.

Weights
These are attached to the front of the tractor. If it is pulling heavy implements on the back, the weight at the front stops the tractor tipping up.

Bonnet
Underneath the bonnet is the engine.

Warning light
Flashes as a warning that the tractor is working.

Cab
This is where the driver sits to drive the tractor.

Steps
The driver climbs up the steps to get into the cab.

Wheels
The wheels on a tractor are normally smaller at the front and larger at the back.

Inside the Tractor

Here are all the controls that the farmer needs to drive the tractor and work the implements.

Steering wheel
Controls the direction of the tractor.

Here is the seat where the farmer sits.

Pedals
Clutch
To change gears.
Brakes
To stop the tractor.

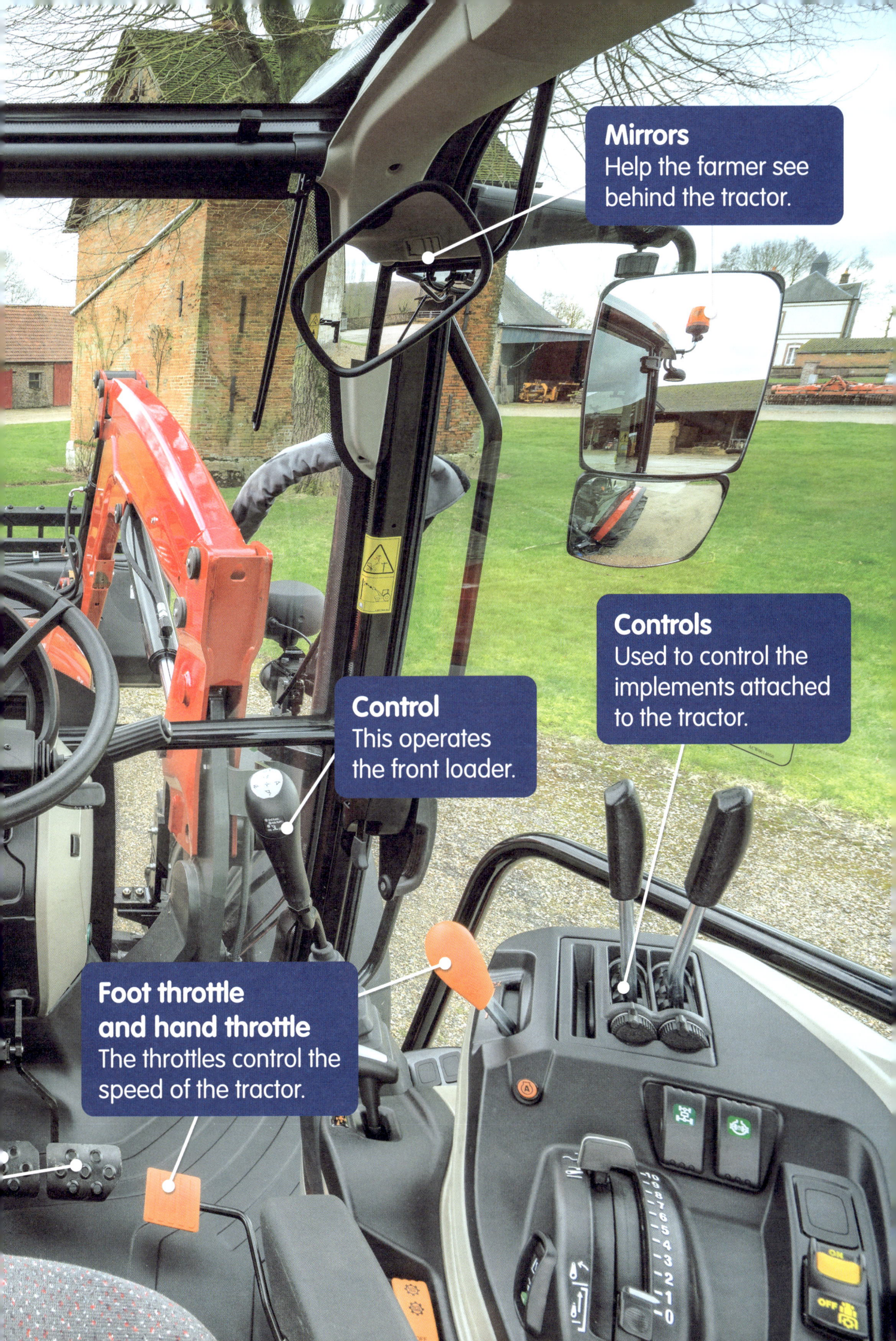

Back of the Tractor

Warning light
Flashes as a warning that the tractor is working.

Rear lights
Used as extra lighting in the dark.

Indicators (orange)
Show which way the tractor is turning.

Brake lights (red)
Show when the tractor is slowing or stopping.

Tyre tread
Helps the tractor grip.

Hitch and link arms
Farm implements are attached to the back of the tractor.

Front of the Tractor

Headlights
Help the farmer see in the dark.

Grill
Allows air in to cool the engine.

Worklights
The worklights are used as extra lighting in the dark.

Front linkage
This is where implements are fitted to the front of a tractor.

Implements

Here are some implements that can be fixed to the **front of a tractor**.

Buckets are useful to scoop, move and carry.

Bucket

Implements are tools or machines that can be attached to a tractor.

Buck rake

Buck rakes are used to pack a crop into the silage clamp.

A bale spike it used to move and load bales.

Bale spike

Muck grab

Farmers use a **muck grab** to move bedding and silage and it is also used to load feed wagons.

Mower

A **mower** can be attached to the front or back of a tractor to cut the grass.

Wrapped bale handler

A **wrapped bale handler** will not damage the wrapping on bales which keep them dry.

Implements

Here are some implements that can be attached to the **back of a tractor.**

A **plough** is used to make furrows in the ground.

Plough

Cultivator

A **cultivator** is used to break up the soil.

Mower

A **mower** is used to cut the grass.

Seed drill

A **seed drill** is used to sow seeds for crops.

Balers

The crop is squashed into a round **baler**.

Rakes

Rakes are used to help the crop dry in a row. These are called windrows.

...or into a square **baler** and tied.

Straw chopper

A **straw chopper** chops a bale into small pieces and blows them out for a clean bed.

Tractors to Tow

Here are some trailers that a tractor can tow.

Flat bed trailers

A **flat bed trailer** does not have any sides so they are easy to load and can carry wide, heavy or long loads.

This **trailer** can empty its load quickly by lifting up so all the load tips out.

Tipping trailers

Livestock trailers

A **livestock trailer** is used to move farm animals from one place to another.

Wheels

On a tractor's wheels are tyres.

Tread - these are the knobbles on the tyres.

They help to grip the ground and stop the tractor slipping.

This tractor has turf tyres which are good for driving on grass. The tread is smooth so it will not damage the grass.

Most tractors have two wheels at the front and two at the back.

These tractors have four wheels at the front and four at the back. That makes eight wheels!!

Caterpillar Tracks

Some tractors have caterpillar tracks. These are good for rough ground. They spread the weight of the tractor to stop it sinking.

These tractors have two sets of **caterpillar tracks**.

Horsepower

The power of an engine is measured in horsepower. Before tractors all the work on the farm was done with horses.

Here are some horses ploughing a field.

First Tractors

The first tractors had a steam engine but these have now changed to diesel engines in modern tractors.

Over the years tractors have been made better and more powerful which helps the farmer to plant and harvest more crops.

They can now be used for more jobs on the farm and so save the farmer time.

Modern Tractors

Tractors today come in all different sizes.

There are **small** ones,

narrow ones,

In the Factory

The different parts are put together in the factory to make a tractor.

1 Here is the cab.

A **chassis** is like the body of the tractor.

3 The engine is part of the chassis – now the cab has been fitted.

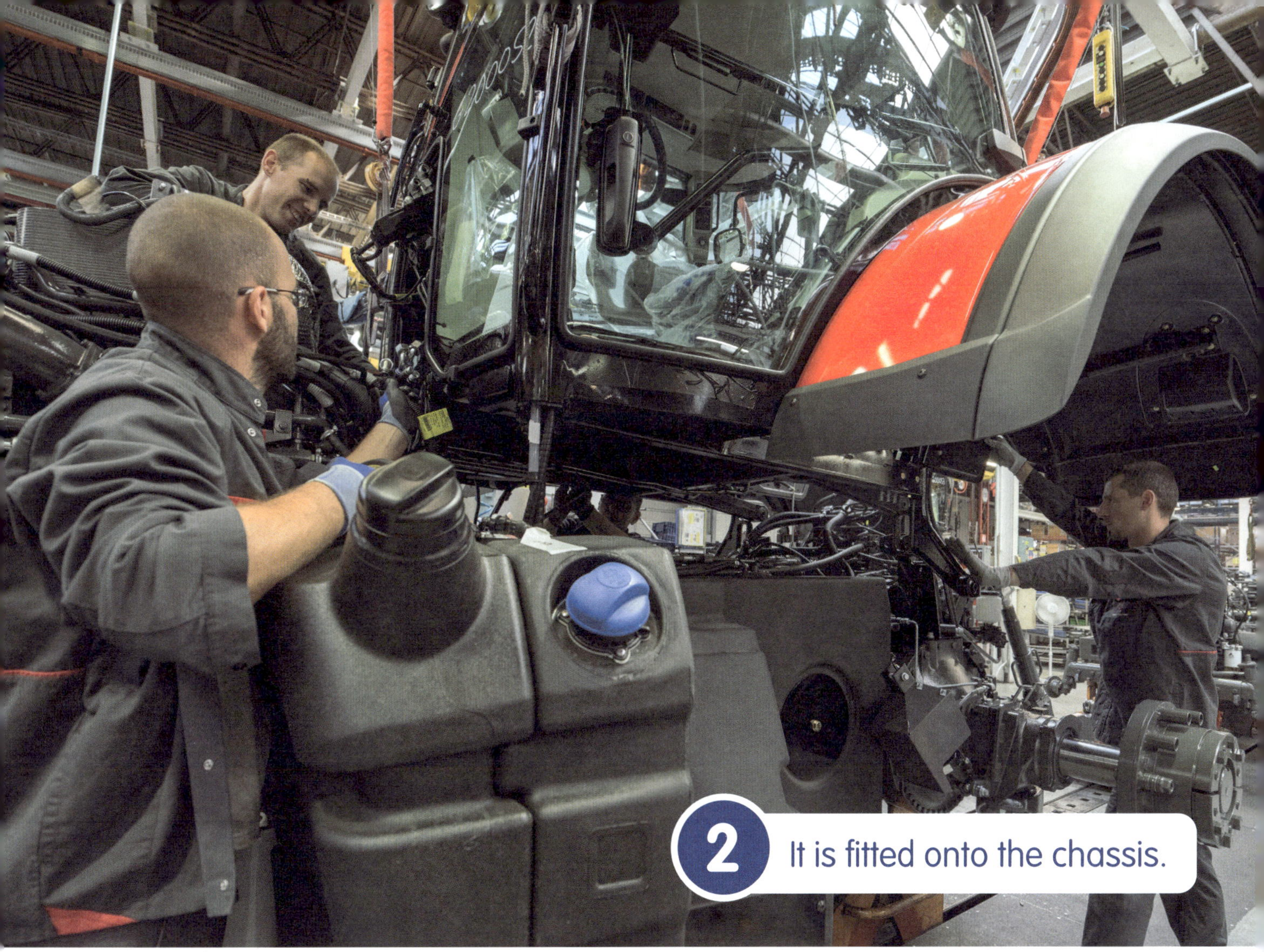

2 It is fitted onto the chassis.

4 The last part added to finish the tractor are the wheels.

5 The tractor is finished.

Now that the tractor has been made it is ready for the farmer to use.

6 Here it is working in the field.

Which tractor would you choose to drive?

I hope you have enjoyed looking at tractors.